TRANSPORT AROUND THE WORLD

TRAINS

Chris Oxlade

Heinemann
LIBRARY

www.heinemann.co.uk
Visit our website to find out more information about Heinemann Library books.

To order:

 Phone 44 (0) 1865 888066

Send a fax to 44 (0) 1865 314091

Visit the Heinemann Bookshop at www.heinemann.co.uk to browse our catalogue and order online.

First published in Great Britain by Heinemann Library, Halley Court, Jordan Hill, Oxford OX2 8EJ
a division of Reed Educational and Professional Publishing Ltd.
Heinemann is a registered trademark of Reed Educational and Professional Publishing Ltd.

OXFORD MELBOURNE AUCKLAND
JOHANNESBURG BLANTYRE GABORONE
IBADAN PORTSMOUTH (NH) USA CHICAGO

Designed by Paul Davies and Associates
Originated by Ambassador Litho Ltd
Printed and bound by South China Printing in Hong Kong/China

ISBN 0 431 13410 3 (hardback)
06 05 04 03 02
10 9 8 7 6 5 4 3 2 1

ISBN 0 431 13415 4 (paperback)
06 05 04 03 02
10 9 8 7 6 5 4 3 2 1

British Library Cataloguing in Publication Data

Oxlade, Chris
  Trains. – (Transport around the world) (Take-off!)
  1.Railroads – Trains – Juvenile literature 2.Railroads – Juvenile literature 3.Railroad travel – Juvenile literature
  I.Title
  625.2

Acknowledgements
The Publishers would like to thank the following for permission to reproduce photographs:
R D Battersby p16; Steve Benbow p14; Sylvia Cordaiy pp7, 8, 10, 23, 27; Eye Ubiquitous pp4, 6, 11, 17, 24; James Davis Travel Photography p18; Milepost p25; PA Photos p15; Pictures p13; QA Photos p20; Quadrant pp12, 21, 26; SNCF p19; Tony Stone Images pp5, 9; TRH Pictures p28; VSOE p22; Science Photo Library p29

Cover photograph reproduced with permission of Alvey and Towers.

Our thanks to Sue Graves and Hilda Reed for their advice and expertise in the preparation of this book.

Every effort has been made to contact copyright holders of any material reproduced in this book. Any omissions will be rectified in subsequent printings if notice is given to the publishers.

Contents

Any words appearing in the text in bold, **like this**, are explained in the glossary.

What is a train?

carriages   locomotive   metal rails

A train can have many carriages or just a few.

The very first railways were just planks of wood or metal plates placed on the ground. They helped the wheels on horse-drawn wagons turn more easily.

A train is a machine that moves along on metal rails. Passengers travel inside the train's **carriages**. The carriages are pulled along by a **locomotive**.

A train driver sits in a small **cab** at the front of the locomotive. The driver makes the train start and stop, and speed up and slow down, by moving handles and pedals.

driver   controls

There are lots of **controls** inside the cab.

How trains work

electricity wires

locomotive

track

carriages

Electricity to run the electric train comes from overhead wires.

The world's first public electric railway was at Lichterfelde, Germany in 1881.

This is an **electric** train. Electric motors in the **locomotive** make its wheels turn round to move the train along.

This locomotive has a huge **engine** called a **diesel** engine that turns its wheels.

This is a diesel locomotive.

Diesel locomotives use a fuel called diesel oil.

metal
rails

cab

Trains long ago

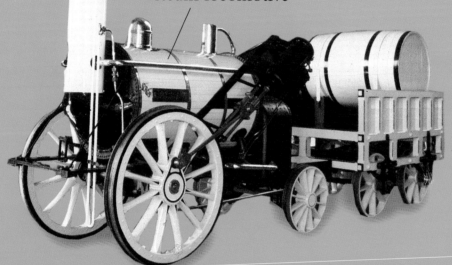

steam locomotive

This is the steam engine which was called the *Rocket*.

Early trains used **steam** for power. The first steam
locomotive was called the *Rocket*. It carried passengers
between Liverpool and Manchester in England.

Monster steam locomotives used coal as fuel.

steam

Monster steam locomotives had very powerful **engines**. They pulled **freight** trains with hundreds of wagons of cargo across the USA in the 1940s.

Steam trains

In some countries, trains are still pulled by **steam locomotives**. Inside the locomotive, a roaring fire makes water boil to make steam.

Steam locomotives are still used in some countries.

carriage

steam locomotive

wheels long rods

The pistons drive these long rods to make the wheels move.

On a steam locomotive, steam makes **pistons** move in
and out. Long rods attached to the pistons make the
wheels spin round.

Where are trains used?

signals

Signals like these tell train drivers when to stop or go.

train

tracks

Long ago, flags and banners were used for signals instead of lights.

Trains can only be used where there is a track laid for them. Most tracks are made up of two metal rails.

Railway tracks go between towns and cities where there are railyway stations. Passenger trains stop at stations to let passengers get on and off.

Railway stations have platforms for people to step on to and walk along.

train

passengers

platform

Trains to work

Every day, people travel to work and school on **commuter** trains. These trains stop at stations to pick up passengers and take them into city centres.

Passengers who go on commuter trains to get to work are called commuters.

This is a commuter train.

train

passenger

platform

Millions of commuters travel on commuter trains every day.

train   commuters

Commuter trains have lots of wide doors so that the passengers can get on and off quickly.

Trains under ground

Underground trains travel through tunnels deep beneath the busy city streets. The stations they stop at are also under ground.

The **subway** in New York City, USA, has more than 450 stations!

electric train

platform

All underground trains are **electric** trains.

Underground trains avoid the busy traffic above ground. They can get very crowded during the rush hour. Inside the **carriages** there are plenty of handles for standing passengers to hold on to.

In Paris, France the underground train system is called the *metro*.

passenger

carriage

This is a crowded Japanese underground train.

Express trains

This express train is the famous Japanese 'bullet train'.

The 'bullet trains' first went into service in Japan in 1964. Why do you think they were given this name?

Express trains whizz along at more than 200 kilometres per hour. They carry people quickly between cities.

This is the front of an express train. It has a smooth, **streamlined** shape. This lets the train slice easily through the air as it speeds along.

Express trains have a smooth, streamlined shape.

Shuttle trains

This shuttle train takes vehicles between England and France.

Channel Tunnel

The Channel Tunnel was opened in 1994. How long ago was that?

Shuttle trains travel back and forth over short distances. One shuttle carries passengers and **vehicles** through the Channel Tunnel between England and France.

Passengers drive their cars on to the shuttle at one end of the Channel Tunnel. They can stay in their cars on the train. They drive off again when the train reaches the other end.

Cars are driven into the shuttle train's special wagons.

shuttle train

Luxury trains

This is a famous luxury train called the *Orient Express*.

The *Orient Express* travels through Europe and Asia. It carried its first passengers in 1883.

Some long-distance trains are very **luxurious**. Passengers have their own **cabins** to sleep in overnight.

On a luxury train, the passengers eat their meals in a special **carriage** called a dining car. It is like a restaurant on wheels. Meals are cooked in part of the car called the galley.

waiter

passenger

This waiter is serving a meal in a dining car.

Freight trains

freight
train

mountains

This freight train carries its cargo through the mountains.

A **freight** train carries **cargo** instead of passengers. The cargo is carried in special wagons. Each wagon is connected to the next one with a hook called a coupling.

Railway tracks are built on a layer of small pieces of rock called ballast. Special freight wagons can spread new ballast when it is needed. A hole in the bottom of the wagon opens to let the ballast out.

ballast

track

freight wagon

This special freight wagon spreads ballast on to the track.

Mountain trains

Sometimes trains are needed to go up steep mountains. Mountain trains use special wheels and tracks.

Can you find the Alps on a map of Europe?

This train is climbing a mountain railway in the Alps in Switzerland.

train

track

snow

Racks like these stop a train
from sliding down the mountain.

rail

rack

Mountain railway tracks have a rack between the rails.
Locomotives have an extra wheel that fits into the rack.
It stops the train sliding back down the steep track.

Maglev trains

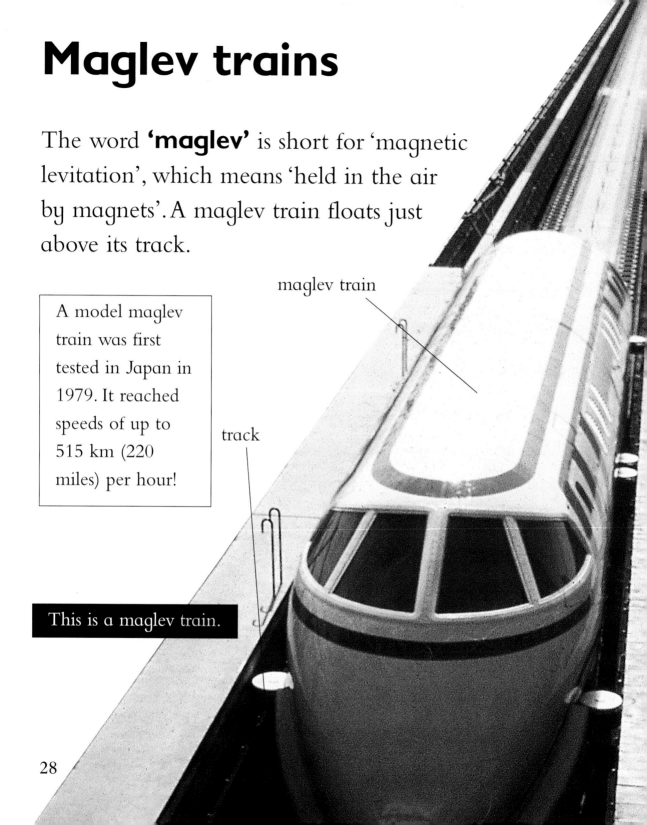

The word **'maglev'** is short for 'magnetic levitation', which means 'held in the air by magnets'. A maglev train floats just above its track.

A model maglev train was first tested in Japan in 1979. It reached speeds of up to 515 km (220 miles) per hour!

maglev train

track

This is a maglev train.

maglev train

track

This maglev train is on a track high above the ground.

There are very strong magnets in a maglev track and train. They push against each other. This forces the train upwards and forwards. Maglev trains are fast and quiet.

Timeline

1800	1803	British engineer Richard Trevithick builds the first steam locomotive. It pulls wagons around an iron-making factory.
	1808	The *Clermont* carries passengers along rivers in the USA. It is the first boat powered by a steam engine.
	1830	The first passenger railway is opened in England between Liverpool and Manchester. The trains are pulled by a steam locomotive called the *Rocket*.
1850		
	1863	The world's first underground railway is opened in London.
	1879	The first electric locomotive is demonstrated in Berlin.
	1883	The luxury train the *Orient Express* makes its first journey between Paris, France and Istanbul, Turkey.
1900		
	1940s	Enormous *Big Boy* locomotives are built in the USA for pulling cargo trucks. Each one weighed 600 tonnes.
1950		
	1981	In France the TGV express train makes its first journey between Paris and Lyon.
2000	1982	A maglev railway is opened at Birmingham airport, England.

Glossary

cab	space at the front of a locomotive where the train driver sits
cabin	private room on a train with beds for passengers
cargo	goods that are moved from place to place
carriage	a long vehicle that rolls along a railway track with seats for passengers
commuter	a person who travels to work by car or train
diesel	type of engine that needs fuel to run
electric	using electricity to run
engine	machine that uses fuel to make a vehicle move
freight	goods that are moved from place to place
fuel	material that is burned to make heat and power
locomotive	vehicle with an engine or motor that pulls carriages or wagons along a railway track
luxurious	very comfortable
maglev	train that floats above its track
metro	the French underground trains and tunnels
piston	rod that moves in and out of a cylinder
steam	water that has become a gas
streamlined	curved and smooth
sunway	the American underground trains and tunnels
vehicle	something that transports goods or people

a b c d e f g h i j k l m n o p q r s t u v w x y z

31

Index

a
b
c
d
e
f
g
h
i
j
k
l
m
n
o
p
q
r
s
t
u
v
w
x
y
z